Orchard Mornings With God

New Poetry by Kerri Nicole McCaffrey

Orchard Mornings With God:

New Poems by Kerri Nicole McCaffrey

Table of Contents for this Volume

To the monks of St. Meinrad Archabbey for a God-centered education, and to Fr. Rafael and Bethlehem Hermitage for helping me to remember the sacrifice Jesus made for us all…

Author's Note

As a youngster growing up in Westchester County, New York—in the foothills of the Catskill Mountains, I was blessed to live in an area with a precipitous hill named Buttermilk, a haunted cliff which Washington Irving wrote about (Raven Rock), and with a farm in my backyard run by the Dominican Order of nuns. When I wander pastures today— with my large field knife swinging from my waist, my muck boots on for mud protection, and my phone handy in case I need to call "Base", I feel more than a little like I did when I played Army as a child and wandered the farm holding my sister's white 'flag corps' rifle and wearing black boots. Vietnam was raging then, and what did I know? Those men coming back—motionless on tarmacs, needed protection. In my mind, I sacrificed for them and for my country.

It was to this same farm I ran when I needed to be alone (a poet starts needing time for reflection *early* in life). We played baseball in the big field and chased red-wing blackbirds in the smaller one. But there were also times when I just went there to run—to sprint from one end to the other for no particular reason, I think, than to feel free. Such habits made me the fastest runner in school for many years.

But it was the convent's crabapple orchard which held most of the mysticism. The convent looked over a pool with little grottos around it and then out to the orchard. Whenever I approached the crabapple orchard in my little boy body, it was with pensiveness and reverence: in spring, it was lit with fragrance; summer transformed it into a quiet crypt; autumn found it drenched in cidery aromas. I didn't go to the orchard much in the winter…I think the tree specters—with their black and ominous arms, scared me.

I loved to sit in the trees and smell lilacs that drifted off the nuns' little mount of prayers. It was in this orchard where I first found God's reflection, as I observed nuns wandering fields and singing psalms. Outside of Eucharist and my sons' eyes, God's reflection in nature is as close as I have ever come to Him. What a gift to have found Him so young! What grace to still find God in the old fields and orchards on which I live today! May my poems help you to harvest His reflection as well.

KNM
8 March 2018

A Poem of Introduction to this Volume

Ecclesial

From deepest dark
and nothing-
ness
from density
of chaos and disquiet
—destiny
and yes
I shake the doubt
like brook otter
at shoreline—

With songs
sweeter than the Lorelei
angels draw me to dogwood's
coral blooms,
blow up blackness
in booms—Ah,
too ra loo ra li.
Bees crawl, slurp nectar
loud
as God's whisper—

The willow bird
—so gentle and green—
sings its best brogue,
"fitz-bew, fitz-bew"
up above—
as other tongues arrive:
"I love you"
"Trust"—
"Do this in memory of Me".

*

Chapter 1
Happily Ever Orchard—
Notes From Childhood

Once, I Sailed the Seas—

When they built the highway by my childhood home
they left a little place where we could play—
a retaining pond island
with prodigal forest
jungle lush and ringed with goldenrod,
purple loosestrife—
I'd often pick some flowers as I roamed.
Construction workers left behind a cement tub
when they were finished, which
(I didn't know its actual purpose at the time)
resembled a boat—
so I sailed it to the isle
—a solitary voyage—
and there, reveled in the quiet
hunted bull frogs and toads
dreamed of other lands and future times.
Five years after we moved
my family drove by the pond,
the tub still there,
moored in sedge.
More recently
I couldn't spot it from the road
—about a half a century now has passed—
I think it's sunk or rusted like a wreck
though once, I thought it invincible.
Could I launch an expedition
(without my sanity being questioned)
I would don scuba mask and tank
explore the emerald waters where it sank
discover something from a time long passed—
an artifact, perhaps:
a baseball or telescope—my white naval hat.
But really, we all understand
no one survives such a sinking—
and though I know my little boy soul
still haunts the place—
I remember once I was a captain!
who vowed to sink with his beloved ship—

Gambol

Entering Pocantico
Fire bells rang their loud
Alarum
And kept up
'Til the church bells sounded.
Then all was as it was—
Pasture walls, dirt roads
And dust.

My mom used to fret
I'd get disoriented up here:
Spinning fields and orchards
—A pale blue dome.
But I lost my way later
In life—
Now I come
To find my way home.

Hail Mary, Full of Grace...

...sometimes, shutting my eyes
I can attempt the old convent grounds:
that place
of fallow fields and berries
sweet
mantra of nuns reciting
their rosary
red winged blackbirds, territorial
dive bombing from above—
lilac
crabapple—
a sandstone greenhouse
at its height—a roserie—
windows now in the shards
of its foreshadowing—

Hail Mary, full of grace,

I stepped without a trace
to a far corner ne'er traveled by any other
I went for all the peace
a 10-year old could muster.
There, a rusted bike
—rubber gone from rim
perhaps belonging
to one of the farmer's kids
whose father worked this land—
before the convent came—
I closed my eyes and imagined
(in that lush green where no trail went)
in that dappled light where all the apples ended,
what that past was like.

Could I escape the buzz and rush of my today
were the seeds and pastures not paved over
—and my verdant spot not a busy parking lot—
I would wonder about that farmer's Heaven:
was it lush, and green, and finally fair?
Now, I'd find the trail that got him there

at the hour of his death, Amen.

First Vows

The crabapple orchard
near the convent's upper field
was full of darkling hallways—
where a suffering child
could find herself
entering the sweet world
of broken bark and blossom
fragmented blue above
and small pink puffs
in the canopy below
abuzz
with fragrance
to heal the lonesome.

She skipped there
then slowed
to enter her cave in the boughs
took vows
sat in the notch of a tree
—good and gnarled—
as the bell rang vespers
she hummed and, still
—sang whispers
to fight off the first of her sorrows.

Seasonal

During wintery play as a child
—snowballs and tree glitter,
the joy
of sledding—
all
would eventually give way
to exhaustion:
panting and sweat
and wet mittens.
Gravely fatigued,
I'd curl up in a drift
—the snow
like soft sheets
conforming to my fetal shape
—warm and willing
to watch others
pass by;
I'd had my time.
Eventually,

the cold grew in me.

Walpack: Keepers

I missed you before you were gone
if that's possible—
I knew long before my sons left
that they were leaving
when they would hunt frogs
at the falls
or snuggle in my lap—
I knew…
Time will not be forestalled…

And Walpack,
I grew up with you—
some of the houses
were still with us then
—wash lines in the wind—
Easter egg hunts in fields
a driveway full of cars for Sunday dinner.
I'd heard by then
you were going
would leave these structures empty
but breathing,
that the kids swimming in the creek
would pack up their bikes
on the back of the '72 wagon
their last shouts,
"Hey you guys! Watch me go under!"
echoing forever
off Rattlesnake Mountain
and back to the Military Trail
like a sound chamber.
Now, many have left this world
and homes are waked
on empty streets—
and as I pay my respects
(forehead pressed on antique glass)
I breathe life into them
and though old and frail,
the very shingles smile.

We carry Walpack's treasure
in the memories we keep
—and though many pass
we are heirs
left an inheritance—
a chance to make it better than it was,
to join our echoes
with theirs—before we too
go under.

The Other Side of Buttermilk Hill

David Rockefeller's *Hudson Pines* farm.

The farmer rakes
mid-May hay
into endless windrows.
Beguiled, I stare
as if these are spiritual
borderlands—
and I am in front
of open windows:
pink fleabane, vetch, wild pea—
cinquefoil, violets, and Timothy.
Remembrances cool and surge
—breezes into a long-closed attic.
There's my son, dear to me—
that's where I grew up
there's our old church
where I heard the sturdy sermons,
"He maketh the grasses
that grow upon mountains"—
And here's the Gate of Heaven
Cemetery (with Babe Ruth's grave)
—green hills and waterless fountains.
Borderlands and their casualties
make us think what we are
and will be.
The farmer bales hay now
and waves to me...

Pining

I remember long ago,
my mother
—her voice so mild—
reciting fairy tales
helping me to place Wonder

Bread bags on my feet
so I could slip on
galoshes.

Now, I've walked deep into evergreens' peace
snow explodes off high branches
sparkling down
anointing the sleeping heads of thrushes.
High above, an emerald canopy
absorbs wintery gales
like ship sails
hundreds of mast poles ache and sway—

I imagine a strapping helmsman there
one hand on tall sapling
bellowing orders to his beleaguered crew—
a drama in spirit and flannel…

But below, a quiet
voice of goodness
I know is always present—
it's just that in this balsam berth
is stillness enough
to hear it.

Attic

Some would say
I simply changed my clothes—
others that I painted
ceilings and halls;
they see I paint my toes.
I think, actually,
I've left unpainted
the pull-down door,
and climbed the attic stairs—
I am done with white-washing
finished with moldings and veneers.
I've gone behind the drywall
where it is good and thick
with quiet—
looking for boxes:
Easter grasses, Christmas bulbs—
one with papers and my father's taxes.
Dark and beam
insulation and dust, too,
dust
and complex webs.
I pull out a strand of lights
plug them in
explosion of blue
holidays past and present
where I've been, where I'm going—
an important light,
deep in the house.

Recess in the Ring

Life was skip and run and shout
in meadows until ten—then,
collection of lilacs
and blue-speckled trout.

At recess we held hands
and circled,

"A tisket, a tasket"—
ten years ago my father died—
days of hazy sailing, stopped.
Here's Mother's grave blanket—

and there, my friends,
her casket.

The delicate balance—
Good Friday and Easter
warm months and winter
ecstasy of the see-saw, and its splinter.

From seed, wheat was planted,
then mown—

I recall another rhyme, chanted:
"Ashes, ashes
we all fall down."

Through the Guides

To Coach Jim Wood of the Berkeley Aquatic Club, and to all of my other honorable, unselfish mentors.

"We all make mistakes,"
said my childhood guru—
now quite famous and gentler
than ages ago.
"It's sort of like fishing," he'd say—
"…pull some line out
push it through
eyelets on the pole—
there, that's smooth."
Then, stiff wind—
knots like a bird's nest
—all wrecked.
Undo what I'd done
flip the bail
spool more line now, click—
and start again.

As for me
I acted impulsively
resigned from a job I love—lost
blue mist and loon song
slashed soul on the knife
of my wrong.
Dazed—a recollection of waves
creaking rowboat conversations,
louder than the world's—
less plastic:
Flip the bail, spool the line;
there now,
cast it—

Hide and Go Seek

As the sun began to set in our little hamlet
"Ready or not, here I come!" Might be heard,
or a can kicked in the street—
a thud-clunking sound
from the period's heavy aluminum—
or a young color commentator
who just hit one long
in stickball—
"...and Mantle hits one *deep* to right!"
If you could walk my old street—
the sounds of the joyous:
"Olly, olly oxen free!"
Perhaps it would be a late June night
for your little time travel
children with glass jars
chasing green phosphorescent
light.
Gradually, as the evening wore on
and darkness landed,
less and less would be heard—
our little groups of friends disbanded
and the sounds of television shows
commingled
with choral crickets.
Gradually, a few grew too old to play—
some went to college
—a half dozen moved away.
And you'd be standing there
on your little trip
wondering what happened to the joy,
how'd it all unravel?
As if by reflex you'd shout,
"Olly!
Olly, olly oxen free!"
Like you were knocked in the
solar plexus.
You'd open your eyes
and be standing
next to me...

The Color of Absinthe

During solar eclipses as a child
everyone warned me
to shield my eyes,
"Don't look at the sun—
you'll lose your sight!"
And now I'm told not to stare at God,
"The beatific
would be too much...
you'll lose your life!"
—they seem so very certain—
Heedless, I roam
and touch the holy curtain
—I'm not the best at listening—
thicket of absinthe
skies
all a rose-blush china
nights of foxfire—
Like a playful child
tempted to locate hidden gifts,
I briefly pause to ponder:
"Should I spoil this big surprise,
I wonder?"
One day will I peek—
and that will be that,
I surmise—
ending this game
of hide and seek.

Sleepy Hollow: Return to Raven Rock

I perch on the edge
of this fall cliff:
—boulder, rose quartz, granite—
the spot's isolated
and in a canyon.
All my fortunate friends travel
to Costa Rica, Phuket—
Seville.
But even without their means,
I tour a more distant land
I can't forget—
where I meet my mother
who sat with me here
when I was ten
drinking Frostie grape
or Schweppes soda.
Now,
winds pulse our clothes
and we're strangely unafraid
of being swept over.
They say it's freezing out
—that I should dress in layers—
ah, text after text
from friends on their phones.
Funny—I find it fair—
as Mother and I peel back the years,
converse—
among the ceaseless stones...

Beverly's Song II

Crayfish creeks
hide and seek
solo hikes,
to find our bearings.

Lilac forests
apple orchard—
wandering Halloween
without our parents.

Balsam, wrappings
—spring-basket blessings.
Dominican priests
—our first confessions.

Brings me to evenings,
my father's chair—
the 10 o'clock news,
Pall Mall and beer.

This home held me
for important times:
JFK, Malcolm X, Martin Luther King,
"Let freedom ring!"

When Bobby died
I walked home with mother
who wept and whimpered,
"...just like his brother!"

Inside, she quivered
as death took its toll,
so I ran to the river
that surged under road

(from where I and my country
never emerged).

Into echoing darkness
great men have gone,
yet waters roll,
and hope lives on.

Leave a Message

I opened the old phone book
as if unraveling scroll—
buried since childhood
now parched and yellowed.
Numbers, rates, codes
hieroglyphs
black and somewhat cryptic—
exact addresses
for all the places I visited
with Mom:
Dr. Clyman's, Lucy's Delicatessen
Orbaek Farm.
It says my best friend lived
at 16 Fay Place,
so I take a chance with this
in Google Earth
and make a flight of fancy—
Now I'm in my old haunts
but seem to do the haunting.
There's 844 Commerce Street
—*Hawthorne Shoes*—
I feel my somehow resurrected mom
hold my hand
as we exit the blue
Pontiac there—
I'm 6 now instead of 54, asking,
"Please can I get some Buster Browns?"
(I liked the brand's namesake
and his pit bull terrier).

"We'll see, honey," she says—
"...we need the need the sole to last."

Suddenly, I realize the oddities—
an urge to buy this antique directory,
the fact that my family's address page
was the single *one* bookmarked
out of 310 possibilities,
and the clear conversation with my mother—
who'd used the phonebook
to make a call.

Halfway Up Buttermilk Hill

...an opening in the trees
forms a promontory
where I can see many miles—
light green pastures turning gold
black and brown cattle dots,
clouds
dazzlingly high—
white as a block of quartz.
Across an unseen river
Palisades, the Hudson Highlands;
subtle breeze
and I am sighing.

I recall playing here
as a child
and not noticing the breach
in sassafras
and scrub oak trees—
drape of mists,
the surreality.
Now I do,
and am tempted to such windows,
for sometimes
they're left open—
Church found them often.*
I'm drawn more and more as I age—
Soon, will I float through one
—scenes of quiet pastures—
and haze.

*Frederic Church (1826-1900), was an American impressionist and landscape painter whose works captured the majesty of the Hudson River area—and God's transcendence through nature.

Sublimation

I walk into clouds
to get a clearer picture
of myself,
like pulling up the covers
when I fell asleep
in our big family—
cave of woolen wishes

and cottony blue quiet.

What did I know about hardship—?
My brother lied to me? School was boring?
A neighbor stole my sled?

I knew my father had stress
I couldn't see—
the five packs of Marlboro
kind of gave it away.
I was joyous one New Year's Eve
when he came home happy
—he'd won the Basket of Cheer.
Soon after, he tried to ease his commute—
the 180 miles per day stopped
when we moved across the Hudson;
I hated the new place
and so,
my first hardship.

In science class today,
I taught about matter
—how a change of state sometimes
brings the nimbus.
This is clear:
one day we'll all change
and bring nothing with us.

Fall, Rise—

The moment my blue step
tentatively touched Raven Rock
the bird's croak
alerted me—
a sudden alighting
high in a hickory.

It tore at a round wasp's nest
with small, raucous roars
and ravenous caws—
then clasped
half the papery globe
in black-ivory beak
and flew off—
bleak as a judge
exiting the chambers.

Since Washington Irving's day
they say the glen is
haunted—
a woman in white
fell here or froze;
people have believed whatever version
they've wanted—
but her screams are heard on nights
when icy winds blow.
Today, a vertical precipice
and deep autumn leaves
hide the glen's rose-quartz floor
and sure lethality—

It is bewitched.

And there is some risk—
but on a day when I'm dispirited
by heartless human words
—I've climbed a cliff—
and seen the ether:
symbolic dissolution of bees' nest
nearness of wings
and feather-black breath—
Far from where I've started,
I've come back blessed.

Rookie Years

"Don't do dat, do dis!"
Boomed my first baseball coach,
his black plastic sweat suit
visible under cutoff cotton pullover—
The smell of sweat was new to me
and it permeated our conversation—
I seemed to catch droplets in my glove
as he lectured me—mano e mano—
out in short center:
green grass, 1960's sky,
Easter approaching...
He spoke with passion
and I trusted and listened
—guessed the sweat was a baseball thing
that made him sort of glisten—
had my first try at reflection...
fact checking
—at success and failure.
With a fungo
he hit me a grounder from ten feet out
—it rolled away from him and under
my still developing legs—
which brought him on me
like a spring squall:
"Aww, you see? You did dis, not dat!"
Don't do dat! Do dis!"
And the whole thing would recur…

Though I never realized my dream
(to play as a professional)
advice, course correction
—everything was simpler
as a fledgling player:
I wish I could talk to that coach today

in the confessional.

As You Whistle In Sleepy Hollow's Graveyard

At ten,
I'd already been exposed
to *Dark Shadows and The Exorcist*
—and perhaps because my town
held Sleepy Hollow,
I began having fitful rest.
One midnight I woke to organ music
and a vision of Dante's Inferno.
If my parents didn't know I was special yet
they soon did,
as I ran up the split level's steps to their room
demanding they, "throw that evil book away!"

I studied religion in college
—befriended a Jesuit from St. Louis—
who told me the horrors of *The Exorcist*
didn't do the real thing justice—

Shortly after the Alighieri incident,
I crossed the Saw Mill River
and climbed Buttermilk Hill
where I walked the carriage trails
of Hudson Pines.
Stepping into mixed moonlight,
I saw the Headless Horsemen
alight on cinder.

Now you might accuse me of being
schizophrenic
but there were wails from the woods,
—screams and moans—
I turned and ran in panic,
plummeting off the Goat Trail
to leaf-strewn dell—
barely escaping the high fiend's hell.

You might think you are smart,
my friend, professing,
"Well, these things don't exist!"

But explain that
to the Jesuits.

Old Art Shops

On a warm June day
when I was eight or nine,
I walked the banks of the Saw Mill River
surveyed treading trout
slow thrust of tail fins
back and forth
twin talisman
in the languid flow.
Suddenly, a woman appeared—older—
I guess late sixties, perhaps—
with wooden easel
palette of colors
canvas and brush and smock
some sort of reading glasses
her hair gray,
with blue bandanna.
I wanted to explore above the bank,
but with her there my way
was blocked.
I was shy and averted eye contact,
but she smiled, "hi"
and, "beautiful day!"
Unresponsive, I peered
at the tools of her trade
and arced around—staring in wonder
at the impression she'd made:
translucent stream, iris flowers
grape vine and willow
—backlit green.
Four decades have passed and I reflect
remembering the lambent haze
of my raspberry summers,
wonder
where she is
—how the painting turned out—
knowing perhaps, I should have cherished
those morsels, now memory.
Ah, maybe in her wisdom
she knew
I'd come to this—
(ensorcelled as I was, already)
and decided to brush me in
that I might look back on one day,
one day—
I am searching for that painting, still.

Moving Boxes

They've been with me since I was a child,
boxes stamped Neptune, Atlas or Mayflower
—always appearing with the suddenness of
finding new land:
I've sailed, am in a new place
and in the basement
they are there,
brown and corrugated
rising like the Cliffs of Moher.
My father moved me untold times—
and I left one college for another,
married, new house, trading shirt for blouse
pants for skirt—this gender for that—
the moving boxes never sated,
never fully unpacked—
always there
in the back of a closet
or deep within an attic
to remind us that things can change
quickly
—and dramatically.
Inside, they hold memories
like a safe holds gold
a cupboard, spices
—like a body holds soul.
Perhaps they are more
navigational buoy
(calling seagull and rhythmic knell)
than any anchor.
I have found myself
kneeling before their contents
just short of adoration,
boxes which are part of me
nurture me
nourish me.
Perhaps more altar
than tabernacle containing holy host
—for altars hold the moving boxes of millions,
Amen.
They are brown and corrugated
stamped Atlas or Neptune or Mayflower
and remind us, always—
that, ah—in this place, we
are pilgrim.

Presiding at the Catholic Burial Rite as a Young Seminarian

It was a hot day in July
when Monsignor asked
if I would do the Rite of Committal—
I didn't even know the family,
but what could I say?
For he outranked me—
just below a bishop
and I just a seminarian
—checkmate—
always something more powerful.
I drove up the urban highway
to a cemetery I'd never seen before
dressed in black
dark sunglasses
collar—
as I walked to the burial plot
everyone called me "Father"
—the sweat poured off me—
and before I began the service
I wished it were already done.
The women wore black skirts
and panty hose
the men, tailored suits,
greased-back hair, and cologne
which mixed with wind
and oriole song.
When all was hushed
I read the rite:
"We commit his body to the elements…
ashes to ashes, dust to dust—"
They wept, they cried: the men
put their arms around the women.
I felt empty and alone
staring at the dark hole
which I knew
was deeper than they thought,
and something cold
placed fingers on my shoulder
trying to assuage
the comforter
who was comfortless—
a single woman
moaned.

Playing Army

I pushed my mom
Through the nursing home garden
Perhaps her last
Spring
While on the hill above
Two boys played Army
Shooting each other
With imaginary guns,
"Pitchoo, pitchoo, pitchoo,"
They sounded
As the unseen bullets flew.
It seems only yesterday
I was them—
Playing near early rose
The crabapple and plum.
Tomorrow, I'll be my mom—
As time explodes
Like unseen bullets
First, observing wheelchair
Then, talked into it
—Sitting—
"Pitchoo, pitchoo, pitchoo."

Questioning My Dad in the Car

The first instance of time's
betrayal
was in 1972,
pulling into
the Thornwood service station
with my father
while asking, "Where's the Esso gone
and why's there an Exxon sign?"
I swallowed hard:
my dad's heartfelt explanations
about break ups and acquisitions
didn't cut it—
so we bought some Esso glassware
and drove back down Rock Ledge Road.
As a child I recognized
the clock's movement
dissolving days easily
as Mother would dissolve powdered tea
into pitchers of August water.

But time had a strong arm, too—
using the larger hand of the clock
to bulldoze any roads back:
the nuns sold the raspberry farm
where I spent hours;
my father dealt the Hawthorne house;
the failure
—and dissolution,
of marriage.
Perhaps Dickinson was right:
how quickly we pass the recess ring
—the children all grown up—
time comes for me in a carriage
where perhaps my father will be next to me
once again
and I will ask him,
"What's this new station—
and where
are the vital signs?"

Surf

We vacationed in Montauk
when I was young—
our colorful camp tucked behind the dunes.
My father always loved it Downeast:
coral skies and cloud plume
a sapphire surf's release and foam—
twilight time with family.
One night, he barbecued strips of steak,
but each time he turned his back
a gull stole the stuff right off the grill.
Furious, he attacked
with spatula and cusses
but the bird alit on distant pole
not caring much.
To my dad's ire,
such disturbances continued
until all his meat was gone
—and what remained
was fire.

Last night, his ghost
floated through my room—
blue wind
on ocean dusk,
or soft hearth flames.
Reminiscing (as I knew I must)
it was the sea I beheld,
the ever-renewing swells—
I saw him with cocktail
—unperturbed—
his new existence pure postprandial—
in the dunes
above the scree.
Later,
I dreamt I saw the hungry bird
upon a pole:
"Are you ghost?" I asked the gull—
which turned its head
and looked through me.

*

Chapter 2
Meet the Pasture of My Church
—Growing in Faith

Early Morning— Ossipee Lake, New Hampshire

The delicious sound of stillness—
not even the lake wakes
a loon
calls ethereal, mystic
and fog is thick

like dry ice
in a cauldron of water—
The moon
dissolves like sugar
in a tangerine tea.

White mists
orange dawn
blue sky
your heart is torn—
but sapphire water is rare.

Waves close, wounds heal
night's absorbed by day—
The universe, my friend, is fair.

Deep Skies

I've been thinking
Of God's grace—the great blue
Heron
Perched upon a tree
Heaven
Come down—
Mystical and free
Echo
Of owls
Three deer staring
From snowy fog—
Land become cloud
The present
Of gradually
Knowing God.

Holy Saturday, 2018

Sadie the St. Bernard
is all senses in the meadow,
snorting, snuffling, wet nose
twitching
with lavish aromas.
And I'm lost
in pretty firs
all a'scent with sap,
fresh smell of springtide—
red pines remind me of board lumber
in my father's workshop.
I'm not sure what Sadie's looking for now,
nosing up dark sod...
Maybe she knows it's Holy Saturday,
—perhaps
we both seek God...

Today, I Resigned My Summer Camp Job...

...in New Hampshire—
told them it was something
I no longer loved.
Truth is,
I miss my kid
like a black bear
would miss her cub.
Now, I yearn
for loons and fog—
that clear blue sky
views of Chocorua.
Memories are merciless—
but I've traded place
for person—
pension
for peace—
yodeling loon
for soul song—
and Colin, baby,
I'm home.

As Kitchen Windows Fill With Light

It's so simple and quiet here—
the refrigerator's hum
(condenser/
coils of copper)
my phone
a poem—
and creak of wooden chair

resembling the Santa Maria...

If there were an eavesdropper
would they hear me
sipping the last taste of *Joe,*
squeezing oranges
—as if I'd scurvy of the soul?
The prow of my elbows
plunged
into a yellow-linen
sea,
headed for Dawnland—

writing
as if this verse
were vaunted
or mattered
to the still sleeping—
and those speaking
Spanish
in their dreams—
like I had found
undiscovered Lorca
when it was never really
that

—just something
more native,
verdad?

Federico Garcia Lorca: accomplished Spanish poet, 1898-1936.

Scents

The last rose you ever smelled
is pressed on page 105
of Jane Kenyon's *Otherwise.*
You adored the color of the Esprit
so I picked it for you in the hospice garden
and you grasped it awkwardly,
enjoying the fragrance
as a few petals fell
from your stiffening
fingers.
Eventually,
lassitude saw you drop it to the floor—
I sensed the gravity,
—that this was not an average bloom,
but a memento, a pink relic, an heirloom.
My sons saw me pick it up
and place it in my short's pocket
only guessing why…
Yesterday, I cried at your funeral—
—memories—
are all I have of you now,
like the scent of a bouquet to the blind…
But tangible indeed is the one charm you chose;
I'll remember you
with this rose.

Cosmos

And even pokeweed berries
are a pretty purple
my soul said—
wouldn't you agree?
Why look how they shine
in the sunset
hanging there
like some wild
moons circling Jupiter.
And what a pasture palette,
juxtaposed next to sweet pea
with its blue sky fruits
much more down to
Earth.
It's lonely sometimes
out here in my cosmos—
Every now and again
I find such a lost universe
as space winds
gently brush blossoms
my vessel drifting…
apples, ripe and full,
fall,
I float
finding sustenance
for the journey
in such sights—
the wagons with their loads.

Soul Lair

Through Holy Saturday fields
rich with sky and sparrow
but not yet full of songbird or buntings
I walk—
tomorrow, instead of Easter egg hunting
I could find ample shot gun shells
in azure, aquamarine
and bright yellow—
steel pellets fledged and flown.
I wave to some hikers
who cross my trail.
And then, like a snorkeler, submerge
into bramble and low birch
sink to regions of solitude,
the kingdom of shade.
Further in
and deep—
to a stand of white pines
where I've never seen
human footprints beneath
(save my own)
—but as far as wild ones go
there have been
lots of fox tracks and quail
the paws of bear.
A few wintergreens flourish
still a month before their flowers though.
One-hundred year-old firs—
I smell their sap
and sense my soul
within me—
Yes, I in the belly of this wood
Jesus in his tomb
or Jonah in the whale.
Reader, I don't know what else
to write
but that to hear another world is food
—another language—
the word of God is good.
Under waves of silence
something speaks softly
behind a muted curtain
like communion in a tabernacle—
I find my soul
in the pith of the forest,
where only dark paths go.

Unintended

She loved summer—
cavorting,
belly flopping
in our chilled lake—
snuffling and snorting
without collar or leash,
head cutely cocked
and *woofing*
at minnows and geese.

One day
I heard a frantic yelp, then
whimpers and whines—
a dog's sure cry
for help.
She'd cut her leg
deeply
on a broken bottle—
perhaps tossed to the water
by a partying teen—
I carried her home
—desperate whispers—
as she bled
almost all her blood.
Weeks later, our miracle
would stand—

'Til she became victim
again
a wordless voice
the first of our divorce
—and its dark, sharp shallows.
I couldn't bring Allie to the apartment,
while Jean got a "no"
from her father and mother.
Unpredictable with others,
we felt we had no choice;
I held her as they pushed the needle
and she looked trustingly at me,
as on the day
I carried her, wounded, from the lake;
I wept for weeks.

How to Use a Prism

Below the cottage
Swift Brook streams
clear as table glass,
dancing with trout.

Silently, I ask
classic questions of discernment:
What would you have me do, Lord?
How would you have my life play out?

He waits in earnest for me to settle—
preparing His answer
in pools of water
that eddy and glisten.

Sometimes, I want to speak to my own students
—but pause
and wait for them to listen—
I smile as I think of these small ones

trying to warn each other—with their eyes—
that I am patiently watching.
At their age
I was the same—

New Hampshire is noiseless enough
for my taste—
I can make my way to loons
singing at God's gate.

It's growing silent now...

gone is the Mexican music on streets—
plump women pedaling avocado and bright limes
in Newark and Morristown
—the barter and banter.

What remains is sun-splotched
pitch-pine breezes,
and cherries which hang
like Chinese lanterns.

How quiet one must be
to hear Light!
Water reflects now,
dazzles bark of beech.

"Shhhhh,"
the girl next to me

once whispered,
"...Teacher's getting ready to speak."

Rescue Dog

This morning, I awoke chilled
and so,
drew a warm bath—
but the tub filled cold, illusory—
as the boiler sputtered last night's
Arctic wind, coughed and broke.
At school, my classroom heater
blew but frigid air;
the custodian couldn't fix it.
Later, I called a repairman to mend
the home boiler
and help me reheat
—I at least held hope—
but he couldn't do a thing.

And tonight, my son invited me
to his home—trying to comfort;
perhaps I can finally sleep,
for the tick's as white as snow
and thickly filled with down—
His St. Bernard
covers my feet—
—instinctual—
as if saving me
from frozen Alps.

The Way

Fogs roll
across meadows
—nuns on a garden stroll.
February's thaw
has settled
—all the coming
gloaming…
A pair of love-struck owls
hoot
softly saxophoning
from blackening cave
of arbor.

The return trail starts
at wasteland's gate.
Someday,
I'll find a light dimension,
puddles full of afterglow
—little pathway stones

to bright salvation.

Centering

Our middle pasture's prettiest
of all the other three
—row of old oaks,
(a little privacy)
for prayer and reparation.
The last of the snows
—which tumbled here in grace—
are melting,
and I'm lost in contemplation
—trying to become
less here—and more
on the other side—
a glint of aqua snow
in God the Father's eyes...

Sailor Story

First snow fell yesterday
and lay overnight
heavy and wet
like a grave blanket—

This morning
it rises to an afterlife
as fog
—hovers for one last look.

I don't know what causes it
to shift—perhaps Mother Nature or God.
Slowly it moves down the street
and away in sweeping sheets—

each house enveloped
momentarily adrift in a world of white
a neighbor's dry-docked boat
could be lost in distant oceans—

I would like to roam such vapors,
wander awhile
as a ship in waves at sea
—perhaps find a lighthouse

and move toward it
vanishing—
Ah, the tales I'd whisper
to a searching world

trying to rescue me!

On The Verge

It was a subtle thing
at those crossroads—
Cold Hill and Horizon
and tulips from Holland—
riding bikes—each with a child
—you took Connor and I, Colin—
you continuing on
to your father's farm
as I turned back to our small house.

At the time, I didn't have energy
to climb the wooded way with you;
—thought it would never come.
Soon after our parting though,
I wondered
how your journey was—
and lost love,
I still do.
Twenty years ago
at the base of that hill
we parted ways
(the divorce came only later).
Sometimes,
we arrive at forks in roads
thinking about nothing
but ourselves
and what *we* think is right—
but after lives of agony
and regret,
realize
all that right
is what we left.

From Junction to Cairns

Thirty years ago,
I fished rivers:
the Beaverkill and East Branch—
ah, spring on the Willowemoc!
then tended to adulthood.
I only got back
to my beloved Catskills
recently—
jade-cool water
dry flies and false casting out
demons
"matching the hatch" as they say
—getting things sorted,
after a life I'd patched and cobbled.

From Shinhopple to Cook's Falls
and down to Painter's Bend,
my grown son discovered today
just how these rivers wend—
the holiness here
that hovers:
mist-draped mountains
feeder brooks like small silver
fountains—
pink laurel
dogwood lining frothy glides
and foamflowers
which fill the spring-glad
glade.

And all the while
a flow and push
and urging
of moss-eyed sages—
who'll carry me
to blossoming shore
where I'll be found by my son—
in awe
and finally—
ageless.

What Makes a Poet Cry

Strawberry blossoms
cerulean sky
olive blossom breezes.
One green thicket
smells like *Honeysuckle Teases*
a childhood lip gloss
I loved.

Violet clusters, dogwood
cherry trees, leaves
silver side up—
sugar maples
with amber syrup
for next year
if they survive
spring and summer
storm and thunder

Such beauty
that I cried today—
the world and woods,
its winds
are singing my soul
out of its den
like a mother fox
—singeing with orange and coal—
pushes out the shy one
to jump and swat the sun.

I'm the climber
enamored with views
told to abandon the peak
for, "It's getting dark
and is time to go..."
—a radical disciple
at the transfiguration scene
(the one you never knew)—
refusing to leave the mountain,
Jesus shaking His head
as clouds of white
engulf me.

What We Mistake for Monsters

On a tranquil day at Ossipee
a fisherman cast his lure
over and over.
Goldfinches began their
undulating flight
as sage flycatcher observed from tree.
Worried about my unkempt summer hair
I tried meeting with two of my lifeguards
when a tiny wave rolled across the lake—
rogue, and about four feet wide;
it pushed toward the fisherman
who watched, but seemed unconcerned.
But we stared in amazement—
convinced of our own Loch Ness.
Later, collecting his catch,
the fisherman declared
it had been a pair of loons
swimming underwater—
and in his best New Hampshire accent
said flatly,
"Some beautiful creatures, they ah…"

How Seasons Start

It is raining out
— October—
they say it's the month

of headless things—
of ghouls and ghosts
and hooligans.
The days were all clouds
and spiraling leaves.
I failed at work
terribly—
there were tears.

One morning
I could not find anything to wear
—not one skirt—
so I wore black pants,
the ones with the hole
in the right pocket. Only
I kept forgetting about the breach
and so, lost many valuable things
as the day passed unseen—
Tumbling away,

I never felt them go…

Conversations at Midnight

I left the sound of highways
And homework checks
Went to where
There were only pine trees—
A smattering of snowflakes
Falling on white, deep silence—
There, I asked the Man in the Moon
Questions.

Dover, New Hampshire—June 10, 2017

I occupy a park bench
by the breezy banks of the Cocheco River,
while across reflective waters,
restored factories are framed by sky
—some at least six floors high.
There's a motif of red and green here—
buildings, park grass, trees.
Fire trucks have responded to a call
and sit out on Henry Law Ave
—their red's surreal
but they only idle now;
perhaps it was a false alarm.
An older man with a substantial belly
reads nearby—
intuition tells me he's kind and calm.
Two twenty something's
engage in bearded conversation—
unwed, they might be monks
—or followers of Nietzsche
saying, "God is dead."
Just now, an elderly woman
in blue slipper sox
rides past in her motorized chair
—quiet float on parade.
Expressionless,
she doesn't look at me
so I don't say hi—
I wish I could have that chance again,
but she's moved on
so I don't try.

Someday reader, you may be here,
but this is what my time was like…
Thinking, *I must go now*—
I watch willow catkins
drift downstream.

Sudden Squall

We were called
and the Sea Ray sped
—its thrust almost kicking me
into the famished lake's gut,
the driver bounce-rocketing us
to an overturned boat
and its weakly-sculling captain
—curses bitter as coffee grinds.
Then, sweatpants off—pale skin—
into ghostly water I went
—which slapped and tested me—
gusts ripping past Chocorua
from cold Maine coast;
whitecaps, bubbles, tangle of lines
the vessel tossing
rocking
like a horse
as I heaped the hapless captain
on the flat part of his hull.
Later, we'd tow him
back in the chop and froth,
his vessel having betrayed him
in the soul of that storm.
But I wondered what Geist
had possessed him
to ever leave home.

Now

To the Blessed Mother…

The sun sets
like a radioactive tangerine—
as if it were grown in an orchard
in Chernobyl or Bethlehem—
Everyone stops what they're doing
to cheer the light—
so kind and unusual
with life-changing
consequences—
for Russians and lambs.

Closing. Light.

Sitting here
—in this quiet house—
40 watt bulbs
small candles on sideboards
Puritanical chairs
lined up
like the prosecution table
in Salem:
bleached clapboard and plain white walls—
I guide words
like water into silver tureens—
they exit my fingers like falls.

Thanksgiving
is tomorrow
and I will be alone
with poetry and prayer.

Paintings here
are ocean dreams,
the seats
like sorrow.
Outside, lilac
stands barren—
its last sprigs
staining the dirt
imperceptibly purple,
while somewhere close
both cut stone and circle…

I sip this life
when there is not enough to
swig—
and pen, as Dickinson said,
"…my letter to the world,"
that someday you may see
I traveled, but stayed still—
accepted my conviction
—that I died,
but live.

Jubilee

Have you ever danced in darkness—
just you, taken a balletic step or two
to see if you could
—if it's inside you? You should,
even if you laugh at yourself
and fail
you will never know
unless
—in the subdued light
of the Christmas tree,
the single blue bulb
shining from the crèche
yes—even in front of that unlikely hay—
you take
your chance.
We all have darkness
waiting for light,
holding on for us
to finally follow stars—
No matter the odds
or how deep the night
—dance.

Summer Cloister

This morning's lake was tranquil,
a blue-green eye
unbroken even by a single loon
or breaching trout.
Six a.m.—
a yawn, a stretch, a sigh—
I guard the *Polar Bear Plunge*
shouts of joy and righteous indignation
at the frigid water—
there will be more such mornings for them
I think—then,
back to silence—
a return to my cabin.
I pass another counselor journaling
perhaps writing poetry.
Legs drawn to her chest
in lakeside woods
and quiet—
from England,
she's ebullient during the day
—full of life
but humble.
I've seen her American friends jest:
"Your accent makes anything sound better!
Say, 'Catfish cakes fa dinnah,'" they bray.
I wonder
if she's found a method to deal with it
—life's blue waters
the quick coming of the cold cacophony—
by sitting alone so early and far from home
learning the silent patois
of mystics.
—surely an accomplishment at her age—
to be such an anonymous shaman,
shedding the eponymous
—calming.

While Haying

My favorite picture
was taken when you were seventeen,
you and the farmer's son
perch like eagles on sere aeries
atop 150 bales per wagon
—in the first field:
Allegheny River and ocher light.
The farmer pauses the tractor
for the shot
a red International
with coughing exhaust pipe,
wind gentling butternut trees—
But in the photo
none of that can be heard—
all is timelessness.
I thought of ordering a copy
in black and white
for the color's irrelevant
only the beauty
the pause
the dirt road leading somewhere.
Besides,
color always fades.
And what of you three
who on a clear June day
paused to pose—
dyeing the air
like water spilled around pennies
on clean paper?
Something will always be left there
—a coppery residue—
your souls connected,
tied to that farm—
like hay bales in twine.
In a hundred years,
people will admire this image
—feel you,
even if they don't look up to see
three blue circles
—brightening the air.

On my first morning in Freedom

...the melancholy call
of a lone loon—
in darkness a lamp—
for empty symphony hall
a tune.
Somewhere
in predawn darkness
a beautiful thing, a sound
long and starry and perfectly round.
Escaping thick blankets
that kept me
from New Hampshire's cold,
I hurried like a child to water's edge,
my soul
responding to its old oboe
(a handcrafted one of boxwood
or pear)—
as first light struck the fuse of day.
I saw it there
among the many mists
trying,
trying to tell me something
in the language of another land—
disappearing beneath black waters
with a dive
resurfacing somewhere
far away—
and unexpected.

When You Leave Me

I will return to the Pemi
And close my eyes
Remembering all your joyous words
With a slight touch of sorrow:
"I can see fish, Daddy!" At ten.
At twelve, "Mommy would love this!"
At fifteen, "Could we buy a house here?"
And now, "I'll miss you, Dad; I return to Tech tomorrow…"
If by God or magic potion
Memories flow like rivers in heaven
I want to stand where this one
Meets the deepest ocean.

Pemi: Pemigewasset River, New Hampshire

Search

To find an owl's feather
we must enter the forest—
I have found such magic
in meadow and wild,
past hemlock branch and breeze—
Deptford pink and winter wheat.
Snap a twig, break black birch
and there is pleasantest surprise—
Open my body
in darkness, bleed my core
and you have entered the forest
rolled the stone—
there you will find a single feather
and nothing more.

After Woodstock

What I do know
though
is that I am resurrected
in nature—
All week, the nails of calumny
treacherous straight talkers
those with filet knives
opening doors
saying, "Please, after you."
In the winter, I go hiking
(I wait 'til after two)
when the sun's ready to set—
berries for wild birds:
reds of dogwood
bright blue from cedars
the orange and yellow
of bittersweet—
like a million tiny sunsets
for the dark thickets.
When I arrive here,
all is somehow healed:
I become more naked,
and connect to earth and sky—
Grapevine
for a crown of sorts,
and thorns to make it real—
there's some wood
across
the way—
and there's a little hill.

Ghost Cat

By the end of the 19th Century, the mountain lion was hunted to absence in the eastern United States.

Lately,

we've had sightings of panthers—
As with bears and coyotes,
these canyon dancers
are all a tip toe back—
I've studied their call
to see if it's so.

Last November,
one screeched
out beyond the balsams—
I'll have my doubters
—but we know what we know.

More rare than catamount
is declaring substance without proof
—in the end, it's tantamount
to all saints' senses
and elicits a world of sneering.

On my darkest days—with doubters jeering:
"He's been extirpated—you walk here alone,"
faith screams clarion
—in the deep woods—
like a lion.

A Fine Frenzy

Consummation
bluest sky kissing bluest
water
while across the Black River—
bells ring the Angelus
in devotion to God's daughter:
Ding dong—dong—ding dong.
Holy little hermits
float across their laura—
I paddle in tangible
transcendence
sky brushed with purple
all week, words have been
hurtful
but they are lost
in this liquid mirror
as if this
sadness
is held by heaven
bruising it, instead of me—
Black River's
still sapphire
—but the vast's
a violet hue—
Perhaps this is madness,
my senses reel and wonder:
How does this happen—
indigo from ordinary blue?
Oh, we are all Helen Kellers
at the well pump—
waiting for our epiphany.

Green

The old spring house
below Maple Sap Hill
was dilapidated—
Still, the water in its plunge pool
was clear as finest fountain—
it's glassy stream
flowed to far off fields.

And there was watercress,
wild as a pub in Dublin.
If one cups the riffles now
it's peaceful
like church psalms,
palms puddled with liquid.

The spring's first keeper
hummed a song
and carried iron pail—
but lightning lit him
one black-clad night
—perfection briefly marred.

Now, this spot's alive again
—indigo fire
inside of stars—
wild otter, hermit thrush
—ring of winter wrens.

If you go there he may speak—
or so the locals swear:
"Keep the water pure dear one
for you now keep the springs;
tend it carefully, friend—
how quickly things can end..."

Rover

I feel alone
I've desired this
and now,
like the moment
a rocket leaves the atmosphere,
all grows quiet—
Unlike astronauts
I was not screened for this
hermit's life
though there should be a test—
spacemen must occasionally
have second thoughts
as they see Earth floating—
Murano glass
in comet dust below—
they'll return to us and oceans
when they need
more oxygen though.
I am a hermit now
and quietly float
about the house
from attic to roof:
I rove each room—
...to look for lost universes—
traversing iris blooms
and stars of larkspur
—blue—
and out of air,
I'll be home.

Glass

In the midst of suffering
the hermit's instruction
is to *join my pain with Jesus'*
for the sake of others.
It sounds so brave and noble.
Livvy's husband George
—a Wall Street mogul—
counseled me once
in deep time of need:
"The way through agony
is with brushed hair and grace…"
told in a whisper while
sidled up to me—
a month later,
he died asleep.

I walk the grounds of the hermitage now
thinking of God:
How my friend Eva's eleven year old camper
had it right:
We're all candles,
but not everyone's lit.
And we're being crucified
but not all confess Christ.
I look to the west as he hangs there
wondering why I even matter—
amidst blood like a sunset
those eyes,
blue windows--
I've so often
shattered.

Twenty-Five Hundred Feet Per Second: On Loss

"A man is not old until regrets take the place of dreams." John Barrymore

What have I wrought?
thought Frankenstein
as he beheld the monster,
and Macbeth—
afraid to look on
what he'd done—
pondered I tonight
under full Frost Moon...
Christ washed sinners in blood
—and Mother Teresa
cared for all she loved.
As children,
we walked snowy streets
to sing the happy
carol—
now though
I wake like a shot
longing for something back
—but the bullet's
been blown from the barrel.

Falling Down, Looking Up

Wanting a place to write and rest
I began driving to a little nook
by Lake Winnipesaukee
—but my aching back convinced me
these bluish waters were too far—
so I tried a park,
there growing sad
to see many happy families talking,
having dinner
—cavorting.
Perhaps I shouldn't have felt such,
but with mine so far away
I was mourning.

So I returned to Ossipee
for the sunset—
yellow, salmon, pink and teal
and realized my faith had lapsed
—that whenever I have momentarily given up,
God's given gifts—
And whenever I've given gifts,
someone else has gotten up.

In This Orange World

...spin me like vertigo
deep in the hills of fall
until all I see
is a tangerine twirl
in the wood—
cold-barrel creeks
stalk of corn and crisp
amaranth apple, sweet
precipice:
—Autumn—
Spin me from your fingers,
vertigo
—like the sleeper trick on a yo-yo—
Let me see the whole
orange world:
madcap maple, quince leaf,
and flume—
then, bring me blossoming
home.

Once...

...when younger and pondering divorce,
I had occasion to cross
a bridge
and its clear water source
where my children would sometimes fish
—or skate in the winter's brittling.
From there the channel flowed
to a lake—vast
and all green rippling.
—I paused—
pure sky and one aureate reed
held my attention—like a sweet
rhapsody—
By and by,
something deep inside began to suffer—
the feeling of deja vu
but with the reel spun forward;
for a glint of time or a second only
I could see the future
—prodigious loneliness and my lapses.
I moved on,
living out what I saw that moment—

On bluest afternoons,
I've gone back in search of
that prescient reed,
which might convey new topography
—a return sort of map—
but the sibyl's gone
and others won't speak.

Space

Whatever possessed me to cut tether,
leave my trained ways
spin slow into the kaleidoscope
that sang starlight
as sirens sing songs?

Join the soft universe!
you encouraged me—
blue twinkling, green comets,
pink nebulae.
There's something you all should know—

I can't breathe...

Oh, Nothing Imported

I imagine France is sunny today,
vineyards pouring off hills.
And Tuscany's all a golden glow,
Chianti in wine glasses
—lovers
hold hands in the rows.

Here, it's dank and chill
rain
falls upon fox grape
which now wears mold
like grey fur—

as bears crouch below.

I've not been to Europe
and probably never will—
its domestication
—cobblestone and burgundy—
the Amalfi Coast...
I wait in thickets
—a wild black thing,

seizing anything close.

The Farmer's Gift

We rock-picked the pasture—
repaired the wall
where a wild stream
entered the pond—
the old farmer grateful for help
but ornery and terse.
At lunch, later,
(I can still recite the miracle,
chapter and verse) —
he told us to, "…go for a swim
—you earned it by every rock
you hefted."

Past Holsteins, Guernseys and Herefords
we hoofed it—
journeyed the dirt road
any impressionist would have
painted
—arrived at a place for which
our day was destined
—we, the somehow sainted.

From promontory pond
I surveyed the old back forty—
orchard grass and blush of Timothy,
violet wind
gentling the hay
toward line of birch—over and over—
like a mother
stroking a troubled one's hair—
breezy words:
Mama's here now, child—hush.

Dreamily thus, I entered the water,
descending through changing hues
bubbles up, body down:
aquamarine, apple-green, and teal
soul flown
flesh sinking—
as my son observed
from bluestem by the shore
—doing perhaps,
his first deep thinking.

A Poet Teaching Science Class

Teaching science class
we spoke of mixtures—
of ways to separate
a solution of saline.

After several days,
clear water was gone
and only residue remained—
a pile of little crystals. Memories

...holy books and hymnals—

"You are the salt..."
—*the water flown to Heaven, somewhere*—
the rest—I thought—
"of the earth."

Jade Farmer

This idea came from a news report of the event.

In Myanmar
an unidentified object
tore into the atmosphere
from deep space
blasting and loud,
a fiery alarm—
an errant rocket stage
—orange dawn and dust shroud—
near the tea-leaf farm.
Portions pierced a jade miner's tent
who sat Indian-style
holding a mint gem.
What to do? He sipped chamomile,
and heft a heavy slag
(the color of a comet's tale—)

The camp grew quiet now
with everyone at the scene—
Daw Ma was alone.
He let others
check on rocket seedlings—
here was an Earthling,
content to harvest stone.

Toward the End of Summer

Camp Cody, NH

I found a quiet place to get away—
an abandoned skating rink
about a half mile from camp—
all blue concrete
and shattered glass—
a letter from a former time
with its Forever Stamp.
I'd go at dusk—
a thoughtful place to end my day,
all tucked
in wintergreen
and loam—
riding my bike there
dismounting only
to push the last
through spongy grass and violet—
but to tell the truth,
the place was mostly silent
save for echoes
and hermit thrush.

One night,
I heard shouts from euphoric campers
in the midst of color wars
—drifting here from Cody—
and I knew their noise
would join this ringing
in the endless bell of time
—that someday
they too
would find this spot holy
when they open the letter
—and I am just a line.

At Jane Kenyon's Grave

"Only a dark cocoon before I get my gorgeous wings and fly..." Joni Mitchell

I went to Proctor Cemetery today—
white-splotched azure sky
and placid,
saw the black stone
of your grave—
(*JANE KENYON*—etched in letters
final,
massive):

placed my writing hand
on its marble surface,
so fine and polished
briefly admonished Death
stared into the dell behind
your plot:
white birch, pine, and poplar
but dark—
like so much black ink
spilled.
From there, mountain views
are wasted.

No one else was present
but soon silence
filled with words:

"There are things we must endure in life
that are all but unendurable,
and yet,
I feel there is a great goodness."

I subsumed these, Jane,
from your earthy breath—
Even in death,
Sexton and Plath
couldn't teach me this—
disappearing as they did
into dark wood depressions,
where Wolffs prowl—
I was buried there once
but exhumed.

Today reminded me
to seek the spectrum—
to live simply and unencumbered
for all our days are numbered—
that black gloves sometimes

have silver linings...

The dirt road runs through the cemetery
and heads toward Mount Kearsarge
I must go now, Jane—
it asks for me
—and what a splendid day
for a bit of climbing.

Wolffs: reference to Virginia Wolff, d. 1941, by suicide.

Soul

Everything's saturated
from snowmelt and rains:
I check the cellar hourly
to make sure the sump
is pumping;
the thing's not clockwork…
Yesterday I went for a hike
—just ticks
and early bloom of ivy—
nothing to really get
a girl's heart
thumping…

But I search

among evergreens—
that quiet fragrance
more delicious now,
their trunks—bright,
strike silence as might bells
at

       r
     e
    t
   s
  a
E

It's far too soon for spring
but gray ghosts lift
from stiff ground
warming,
as some mist rises from beneath
my jacket
—like an early warning
oh!
happy ether.

While Snowshoeing

Collapsing on a drift of snow
I savored singular silence.
By and by
a flock of crows
whirled overhead—
black headdresses
whipped with wind
(as if myth or holy
scripture)
—cawing of me, surely,
without using cellphones
or computers;
wondering if I was food
or a kind of intruder—
Undeniably, I'd become a brushstroke
in their picture
disconnected,
but connected—
only a half back home,
yet here,
whole
Singularity is coming, they say
—man's body merged with machine—
but what about
our soul?

Granite State

There's a birch tree in my window
just beyond the screen,
white trunk of eternity—
leaves of fresh lime-green.

In New Hampshire
it's exactly what one might expect:
forest straying to cottage
shelf of books by the sil
bright birch/singing brook—

Someday, I'm sure,
there will be a window
and I'll be in a state
where I don't quite know
what to expect.

May that place rival
these good woods.

Looking for Moose at Midnight: New Hampshire

Connor and Colin—I'll be there for you…

Passing a few cars just beyond Lincoln,
things were routine:
high beams, headlights, high beams—
panning for antlers or nine foot eye shine
to no avail
as temperatures dropped and altitude
sailed.
We stopped at Kancamagus Overlook
(so beautiful in *a morning* glow).
Now, clouds wreathed all
and the car's lights
projected our nimbus shadows
high above the valley floor—
like floats in some dark parade.
My son kiddingly formed "Christ Above Rio"
and I made a writhing ghoul.
Though unspoken, we appreciated
there might be few
such moments of togetherness left—
as each one of us in turn becomes
backbeat and soul:
Time playing steady
percussion.

We tried to pinch the clouds
but they were evanescent.
"It's so weird," he laughed—
"I know they're there
but can't touch them!"

Recycling Buddy Tags at the Camp Swim Pier

For fourteen days,
small plastic tokens
helped prevent loss of life—
sky blue
and sized like silver dollars,
they were precious currency—
for a missing one
might mean a camper
had slipped
under black waters of the lake—
our gravest emergency.

Acetone wiped clean the previous session's
camper names—
permanent marker drew the new.
Days of summer memories
—forming bonds with each child—
and then, every letter gone
with pass of chemical
and cloth—
like wave of magic wand.

Kate from the Ukraine cried the night
before her dark flight home,
saying how much she would miss me
and Camp Cody—
sobbed she'd probably never be back.
Oh, how she hugged me and wept!

As I went to blot her tag,
something stopped me.
I wrote a little poem on the obverse
with fine-point Sharpie,
(her name on the front intact):

Remember camp
And the memories it gave you,
For when life gets difficult
They may heal or save you.

Simple lines to preserve a life
someday,
written on small, round
tag.

The next morning,
I woke early—
and packed it
in her bag.

Loons

This morning
...we had loons—
they joined my lifeguards
who were doing morning chores:
fixing buoys, moving lines, tightening bolts on the dock.
The teens watched reverently
as the elegant birds dove
and rose...
Dove—
and rose...
Having them this close
awesome, but odd.
One was awed
by the bird's red eyes,
another, afraid she'd be bitten—
but even she studied
the black and white birds
with whom all were smitten.
Alas, clouds grew massive
and our loons flew off—
an odd sort of life, I thought,
the constant up and down—
diving and rising
rising and falling
—the supernal calling—
mystique mixed
with black and white.
I am sure there are many ordinary days ahead—
but this morning,
we had loons.

Good Friday

It was now about the sixth hour, and there was darkness over the whole land until the ninth hour, while the sun's light failed (Luke 23:44-46).

Walking near tall timber
pear blossoms and lamb's ear
I am drawn
to distant fruit tree
blossoming
a few fields over,
pink and fancy—
Below stands a white horse
as if an impressionist
staged subjects
for painting—
Yet the air's surreal—
neither movement of wind
nor horse panting.
It's 3 p.m.
and something's not right—
the willow and cherry
are weeping.

Recluse of the Pines

Shrouded
in the green-pine wild—
the last of the snow
having finally fallen,
I lean against spruce spires
and listen
—motionless and muted—
each of the ancient trees
creaking in wind
sometimes together
then, alone—
exactly like doors closing
in a dark, old home;
these balsam hallways
are haunted—
some of the noises
like an elderly one, calling—
phantoms in upper rooms
visitants below.
And I've been adopted
—a sable-haired ghost—
pale and thirsting
peering through boughs
—perhaps at you
who wander white pastures
frail and searching—
I'm like an ancient one
calling—
the last of the snow
having finally fallen.

At the Sod Farms in May

Purple perennials, sweet potato vine
little lilacs
salvias, bright as valentines—
I knew I would miss Jean
coming here without her—
this was an annual event
when we first married—
later, we'd bring the kids.

The northwest hills surround the place
and the valley's like Nebraska
long and flat
greenhouses resemble barracks—
sod farms with soil, rich as coffee
and black.

My son's older now and browses with me.
We buy coral bells, wine rose,
a morning glory.
But I can't buy back the years—
there is nothing perennial
about a lost marriage.

Deep breath, a sigh
the sky has a storm in it—
my soul, some brokenness.
The cold front's clouds
are perfect periwinkle—
I buy monkshood,
wander the flowers…

Posting a Picture to Facebook...

...of the dulcet peace
in a knoll of pines—
I found
all the viewers
—a kind of selfish lot—
wanted its location
so they could retreat there
as I had done
which would, of course,
have ruined the spot
among fragile wintergreen, violets,
and white wood sorrel—

Such peace is not sought out for fun—
it's fought for
and won.
My life has been a war—
I have lost whole brigades,
nay, divisions—
finally now, the laurel!
I've sheathed my blade,
steeled my will.
Please, I think,
at least now grant me
the solace
of this one hill!

So I lied
and told them the spot
was in another state:
Connecticut was the charm.

"Go out by Litchfield and you'll see a farm—
travel by the pasture and the herd of cattle
past the swamp rose and the mallow,
and there you'll see a grove of pine."

May this quest be the flashpoint
of a long-neglected inner quarrel—
(for I'll not abide with sloth or stolen valor).
Meantime, will I sit and dress my wounds
for I am in this chancel now
and finally know the sacred cardinal.

Finding Meaning Along the Terminator Line

The day is gray
and set with cold
so I walk from bog to far field's
edge,
eyes lowered—looking for something
more interesting
than dying light, frost-lick, and sedge.
—A pause—
I kick something soft
a dead mole, velvety fur still warm,
giving me something at least novel—
head and nose
a little cake-icing nozzle,
rake-like feet.
Preserving its dignity, I cup my hands
and perform the tiny burial—
coffin of soil/pall of leaves
Nearby, a pale pile of bones, perhaps
rabbit kit, woodrat or vole

—how vacant things look without the soul.

Heading back,
the sun's behind my shoulder—
chaos of color
brushed by some spectral artist—
or space arsonist
sparking blazes to end his dolor.
And who knew the brittle-bark of cherry
glows ultramarine
in these twilight beams?
An Eastern meadow, suffused
in dusk's last luster—
resplendent pine
guardian of the light/dark line—
Oh, blue-stone sky!
I drink in the aerial—
Bones, bones
why—?
What a day
for that little burial!

Summer 1999: Working for the Tree Company

Operating the chipper
my pace became pushed
the sun, so bright—
I wasn't sure what affected
my vision more—
the salt from sweat
or light—
The limbs coming in
had vines of poison ivy, twisted
fox grape and bittersweet.
Dreamy from engine drone,
monoxide and breath of pines,
I did not see this skein
or that I was tangled
in the thick viper,
as I fed its leafy head
to a steel beast.
Suddenly constricted
between vines and machine
I fought fruitlessly
but slid toward the cipher—
my chance at emergency shut off
beginning to fade—
then, silence

as the crew chief cut power
upbraided me
like a Marine recruit in Basic—
In quiet moments today, the realization
that I'd been spared the rare fate
of ending in splotch—but not by much—
saved from mulch,
pardoned from young children
saying final goodbyes;
nanoseconds from soul being
extracted from blood and body.

I recall Mother hand-pressing oranges
in the hazy memory of summer kitchen—
the bright liquid gurgling out,
while comet-shot citrus
scaled a depthless ether—

Crossing Pasture Walls

Tonight's sunset
was multi-colored stripes:
violet, orange, vermillion—
Cold beauty, still sky.
I miss the bergamot, the violet—
the wild purple trillium—
and really, I am not sure
where they've gone or why.
For now, dusk must suffice—
I turn toward home
cross the broken pasture wall;
my boots thump round fieldstone
as I heard deer hooves do
just yesterday—
The sound connects me
to the earth—with farmers
who placed these rocks
and crossed to watch
sunsets long ago—
who were buried once in blackness
(hoped for lilac and hollyhock)
and rose, I trust,
in spring.

Visiting Eagle Pond

I came to Wilmot
to feel your spirit
and see imagery—
to hear things you once heard:
July's bright breeze,
the blue pigment of Eagle Pond,
campers' voices
inspiring poetic lines—
It's just as you left it, isn't it?

Thus, began my search—

Hayfield, peonies, barn—
pear tree, farmhouse, birch.
Somehow, I feel connected
though you are over two decades gone.
I pause here, observing—
as you once studied Camp Evergreen
mining it for themes—
as perhaps Donald Hall now minds me
wishing twenty-two years
be taken off a clock
—or added—

Voices from Camp Evergreen
emerge
—drift across lily pad and railbed—
but I can't make sense of the lines,
standing here all feeling
no words—
as if we meet at some windy opening
where stained glass has been shattered
by stone—
you ask me how I am
—and shocked—
I can only respond
in poem.

With My Sons—Hockey on Thunder Mountain Lake

For Jen Wycalek, a friend--even in the midst of thunder.

Six degrees and I skate
in coat of eider down—
cherishing this time with them,
for they are older now
and almost gone.
They argue, as they did in younger years:
"I scored!"/"No you didn't"/ "Yes I did!"
and truth be told, I don't mind anymore—
for time's a fading symphony
and this but crescendo—
Soon will I skate here alone
—if I am game enough—
perceiving echoes
of these last notes.
Who knows
if they will soothe or sear,
perhaps they'll cut.

I watch as they skate away
to retrieve errant puck. Quiet grows—
distant caw of crows.

A snow squall crosses the Delaware,
invades the ice with loveliness—
all is white above and blessed
then, moves on—
Twin snow devils
writhe thirty feet
into the air—
If my boys vanished
as these twisters passed,
I'd understand.
I think they will go in spring though,
dear reader,
in gentler, unnoticed winds—
as once dandelion snow
clung to the plant as you left for school,
and was gone
when you came home.

Ossipee Lake

Sapphire pendant
in China bowl—
emerald brilliance
of surrounding mountains—
this lake's an old soul
—such resilience—
quavering loon
eagle's dive
and midnight moon.

Thoughts on the Kate Sleeper Trail, New Hampshire

The lake sleeps
under blankets of mist—
loons rest,
waves cease:
primrose shut,
and moon peaks.
Mt. Chocorua and The Sleepers
are silhouettes of behemoths.
Dawn will wake these
of the silent granite, honed
—as paint wakes a dusty palette—
But who will stir you
who rest in pallor
under such dark stones?

Early Hours: Ossipee Lake, New Hampshire

Across silent waters of green chiffon,
brightly colored buildings
glow like Oslo
or a colorful village on a fjord:
red barn
metal roofs all blue and bright,
clouds infused with tangerine light.
Sunrise is other-planetary here—
as if this were a separate land:
I enjoy my first taste
of morning.

Transforming,
I shed a small, temporary tear.
Though I know better,
it feels like heaven's arrived,
and this is my chance.
Each day, I do my best to be ready—
(to love God and dance).
A motorboat breaks the calm,
speeds away from distant pier
as a joyous girl's voice rings out:
"I think the ladder's down."

Indeed, I think—
perhaps it is...

Evening Forest

As I walked into the bright blackness
lilac, lily, catmint
breath of unseen blossoms
bray of distant lamb
gamboling the pasture,
I think of sacred things:
waterfalls, fox eyes, the words of my pastor—
take time
go to a distant place of
silence
wants
nothing more
than your light

brightening the blackness.

Leaving the Castle

I walked in fields with him
washed in falls
ate fresh apples
in the early orchard
lay with him in wildflowers,
held his sword—

Each evening we admired Heaven
--its chips of light
every now and again
a star falling—
like a sequin loosening its mooring
from dark silk blouse.

We picked out our future
—a planet
or swirling nebula—
our starry house.

Here is my knight;
look at His shining armor!

Blue Sky and Bittersweet

Blue sky and bittersweet
everywhere I looked—
my neck sore from staring up
at the ringing canvas—
red pine and birdsong and field—
rich as spring in Kansas.

In all the woods there were signs:
last night's attacking owl
lost a feather to thorns—
winter wheat,
pushed down by a herd
of slumbering deer.
Though gone now,
I know these creatures were here—

I circle warm meadows over and over
like an attentive fox—
mild breeze, blue sky,
and bittersweet
inform me—
I just missed God.

And deep inside I know,
it is not all this beauty—
but Him I seek.

Traces

Now the field
is thick with thatch—
my feet sink in it,
fescue, blue and soft
waves
in late spring air;
a meadowlark sings
from an old power pole.
The telephone wire
to a long gone farm
hangs cut and limp
pulsing now and then in breezes
after a sixty-year lull.
One can still see the pasture clearing
(though saplings mar its middle)—
there's a busted silo
without its winter wheat,
and here's the barn floor—
its trough feeder broken
into scrap concrete.

Trefoil, clover and vetch
blossom all over—
this farm's been taken back.
A fellow in black had the winning bid—
they say his name is Time.
I swear I hear voices:
are there words left in that line?
"I'd bid my life!" swings out
above the driveway gravel.
Too late though—
the auctioneer has slammed
his gavel.

The bird continues its dulcet hymn—
a sea of fescue rolls in wind.

Afterglow

Thanksgiving fields are lovely
barberry and bittersweet,
musk and fragrant fields—
the spice.
Sharp pines
a hundred feet tall
green spires in fading blue
growing in holiness and rich loam,
dying bracken—princess pine—
while in distant hardwoods
young coyotes cry
by the black-blessed pond.
Everything bathed in twilight,
—soft pink glow and orange—
Tree silhouettes
—spindly fingers—
always reaching for something
I know is there but have never seen.
Shades of grass and shrub
golden and brown,
nothing drab, much in bronze:
the sunset—an iron pail
of cool water and zinnias.
Lately
the world's been whirling with color
like an out of body experience;
I think about each scene of my life
as I walk and float—
as if in some audition
a self-taught releve, grand jete
along the restricted area
by the thin partition,
these words my note:
I feel so alive,
but on such hikes
am close to dying
and want to go—

Nor'easter: Walking the Meadows

The Nor'easter of March 2, 2018

...and the cold and the snow,
—the wind how it blew—
I needed love in this storm
more than I knew.

Ninety year-old red pines
snapped in half
concussing the ground,
gales like circling coyotes
backs arched
florid tongues—
tails hanging down.

Still the storm raged—and our Father
it was nearly noon—

...I found a shrub strewn
path not far
from pith of pine,
secluded—all lacy
snow
—like drapery
or dress,
like I was about to be wed
and this my trousseau—

I knelt there to pray
but God spoke to me instead—
covered me in white
from eyelashes
—black down—
to fur-lined toes.
In the breeze
I professed my love—
"Shhhhh," He whispered,
"I already know."

Every year...

...the Christmas tree's
a universe of lights—
An ant in the evergreen
once mistook it
for the constellation Orion,
climbed on a sapphire orb
—thinking itself a pioneer—
and was hailed as hero,
falling back
to floorboard colony
through burning lights,
and sticky atmosphere—
bouncing off the roof of the nativity—
splashing down in the bay
of the Bengal cat's bowl.

Later generations would see the naiveté
of this one and its brothers,
confusing tree for
other worlds—
as once we had Flat-Earthers.
But you couldn't blame this ant
for seizing its day,
so it made more missions
discovering its Cosmos
originated
in a black hole with water,
striped comets
with hooked tails,
and the red planet
Apple 1—
which had an edible core.
The ant enjoyed notoriety
and died in the line of duty—
performing the first spacewalk
on silken tether—
Back home,
horrified millions watched
as a fanged alien with numerous legs
envenomed their hero,
wrapped him like a mummy—
floated him
away.

Today, more sensible ants know the truth—
dare to a star at the outer edges
with a peculiar habit of blazing
for only one month
each year.

Sylvan

Snow and snow
white as light in the eye
when you looked at the sun as a child—
(though told not to).
And I went deep
beyond today,
followed fox tracks
taking me further and further
away
through a bobwhite-whistling wood
where I was accompanied
by the Irish-haired spirit
of that wild dog,

left in a field
of copper-colored grasses
and rose gold,
with snow on pines
and in the passes
—this place grows souls.

Last Family Vacation Before a Transgender's Divorce

Santa's Village Jefferson, NH, and the White Mountains

We parked in that old macadam lot
—a view of New Hampshire—
Mounts Waumbek and Weeks
and in the bright distance
Mt. Washington
hiding its snowcap and sleet
—behind a veil of late-moving clouds—
walked across US 2
all of us holding hands
bought tickets
from someone dressed as Mrs. Claus;
the boys were shy—
the youngest nuzzling your side.
Later, they posed with a plastic elf
which held a giant measuring tape—
one son about three feet
the other pushing four,
and you
chortling at their cuteness—
though you knew the weather
and I,
still a man,
wore crew cut hair—
always floating in front of you
nimbus and sad.

But we acted as if Santa were here—
as though elves were real.
I took the boys on the log flume
arms held high, we screamed,
laughing as we dropped.
I hid it all so well,
one last time wanting us to seem
the model family.
After lunch, we took the cog railway
to highest peak—
you tried to keep us warm,
woolen blanket
red checked and plaid
which just covered you and the boys
as we chugged into clouds
into a landscape more and more
transformed
by coal smoke and ice,
the boys beginning to chill
in the unexpected weather.
You stayed warm for them,

your eyes pleading
—as I grew numb—
actually thinking
that killing part of myself

might somehow
make this better.

Tribute Videos

So many funerals
so many dead
pretty piano and violin music
the corpse's life flashing
on computer screen
birth, children, the day he wed.
It's my favorite part of the death—
this celebrating life.
Every morning now,
I hear such music in my head
—a reminder—

I remember grateful scenes:
baseball in the cut corn
my sons' hazel eyes
love and light
deep green pines—
You'll enjoy my movie when I am still,
but I'll make the film now
and live—
precious days
and love,
symbols
high tides and low
—water
and sieve.

Summer Camp: First Night's Fire

He stayed away
from the rest of the campers,
who sang by flames at the beach.
Like some kinship of porcelain—
or coyote
softened to look for handouts—
not fully trusting the fist
in which they're offered.

"Perhaps he's autistic,"
I spoke to his college-aged counselor—
"he seems so out of reach."
Smug in my knowledge of such things...
We looked toward the teen
who leaned against tall birch—
studying the waves with thirst.

On the last day of camp
he spoke to me in the lunch line:
"Sometimes, I get sad around water—
my dad would always take us on vacation
to Squam Lake—
he died there, suddenly,
two years ago."

It was then I realized
my diagnosis
had been far off target;
he was clearly not autistic—
just missing a lost father.
James was not *on the spectrum*
but on a voyage through it—

We are all sailors
journeying past
remote meridians:
this is the point that's salient.
Now and again
we climb the crow's nest
as if on a rescue mission—

stern in New Hampshire
prow crushing
toward Reunion Island.
Yes, at some point,
Death
makes us all navigators—
serious and silent.

Morning of the Blue

I opened my cabin door
trying not to wake the girls—
it squeaked on rusty springs
but I softly latched it closed.
As soon as my feet hit the ground
I saw the lake shrouded
in mists white as eider down
floating clouds
like dry ice in Halloween cider
—a cauldron of hues,
without a single sound.
I ran past each lakeside cabin
faster and faster
like I would miss heaven—
like gates were closing
at a railroad crossing.
I ran out on the old dock
fifty meters into fog—
all was azure above
and orange where the sun struck
clouds
—my God!—
just as I'd pictured
eternity:
ultramarine water soft and soothing
nimbus-blue like cotton candy—
and from deep inside this sweet surprise
—a loon called—
and moved toward me,
fluting.

The Day Came Lightly Dressed in Green

I drew a rainbow on the board,
a wooden treasure chest
at its end—
with a fragile leprechaun guard
I'd purchased at a local shop.

At lunch
a colleague betrayed me

and after, a bit shaken,
I dropped the leprechaun
on the floor—
an emerald wave of shards.
Still, like an automobile's
radio after fatal collision—
its music box lay in the carnage
playing on.

Each student received a candy
from the little chest—
oranges and berry
—tart sweet apple.

And later, full of heavy things,
I hiked:

sugar maple, birch, and hemlock—
cherry, poplar, and pine
the birds astir,
ringing.
A crocus emerged
before the sky broke open
with violet rain.
Regardless,

I found myself reciting poetry,
singing—

What Needs to be Said

When my mom was in her fifties
I was driving in the car with her
(a brother or sister there too),
and though I don't know what spurred the conversation
she asked that we promise
never to put her in a nursing home.
We all shook our heads
assured her
told her it would never come to that,
like departing sailors
trying to convince wives
they'd never be swallowed by waves.
In such a home last year, she died.
As I scribble this, I'm in my fifties—
and starting to feel the first chop of age—
its froth and white caps which have seen my sons
become more distant
girlfriends, college, jobs—
and I spend more and more time in the widow's watch.
I thought I should say to them:
"Always, please! Save some time for me!"
But I knew they'd respond, "Sure Dad," reassuring me
it would never come to that.

Why I Walk

I grow more and more reclusive
and am okay with that,
except for time's reminders:
waterlogged baseballs
lost when they were ten;
a tree now barren of
their first deer stand;
a plastic egg from a long-ago
Easter, never found;
some shot gun shells,
and a kite string, unwound—
its colorful treasure wriggled to sky
—like a fish off hook swims
back to sea.
Time, the sweet meat of almonds,
once nourished us.
Now shelled,
these halves
remain.

Roseate

A poet trying to find the right word…

Dappled, stippled, dimpled and spotted—
freckled, blotted, speckled, and mottled.
Flecked, blotched, spattered, rosetted,
pied, patchy oh, and dotted!

Splattered, marbled, bespeckled, brindled
studded, sequined, dashed, and pock-marked—
ah, so many colors mingled.
Pinpricked, blipped, and polka-dotted!

Dabbed, peppered, patchy, dribbled
flowered, speckled, sprinkled, splotched,
star-filled, montaged, spangled, dipped,
mosaicked, swabbed, light and shady—

Higgledy-piggledy daubed and daisied.

A Leaving Psalm

I sniff ruby bee balm
bright and blossoming
before driving to New Hampshire
for the summer: "…beautiful lake camp with salary."
So I took the ad's offering.

Perhaps I feel the fragrance I inhale
will keep me with you,
—though I know the truth—
I miss you, and the car door
isn't even shut yet.

Later (past Hoosick and Rutland),
I drive due North, and the culture's changing:
Cider Doughnuts
Maple Latte
Vermont's Best Cheddar!
Every sign brings pain,
like leaving a galaxy and passing planets.

"It's just for the summer," a friend chides—
"put on your big-girl pants."

The Granite State welcomes me with no sympathy.
It's a simple life reality:
I'm sad
because I don't bring you—
More miles pass, distance, strange signs—
Whisper of Ghosts Vineyards.

Blinking

We pull into the hardware store's
gravel lot
and my relative's embarrassed by me—
tells me to wait in the car.
At the lifeguarding class I'm taking,
I try to give the high school girls their space
as we change into bathing suits—
some glare at me in the corner,
one whispering, "Come on girls, he's a bro—"
Later, I hear them whisper,
"It's disgusting."
And today at school
a substitute to whom I'd never related my story
said I must be a brave person to,
"You know, do what you have done."

Inner thoughts: *I'm not fooling anyone…*

I feel alone—as in a skiff at sea
doing an Atlantic crossing—
truth is, I want to turn back
but told everyone I was going.
Scripturally: "For which of you, desiring to build a tower,
does not first sit down and count the cost,
whether he has enough to complete it?"
Collides with, "If you had the faith of a mustard seed..."

God, everything is rising:
the waves whip, the risk,
the whitecaps like froth
on a wolf's lips.

Coleridge: would say
that eleven years ago
I shot the albatross—
today, I bear it like a cross.

The water's black beneath me now
and I'm adrift at sea—
the wind whispers its "disgustings"—
I wait outside the hardware store

blinking at ski slopes
where they're finally blowing snow,
sunset flames the pines—
it's beautiful.

Dreaming of the Country

I'm leaving the city today,
for farmhouse and flowers
ta-da—
instead of crowded parks—
pastures and sweet honey bees.
Forget the train and alarm
—pour some rose-petal wine
whinny of dry-board barn
—sky and radiant breeze—
sunshine, cemetery, script
—all the years I've missed
repaired like broken fencing
out in the old back forty—
Breath for that worn house:
chimes and paint and porch—
kitchen window, periwinkle sheers.
I'm leaving the city today,
of course
—and I will see you there!

Nights

I am getting drunk on moonlight
Wiccan ecstasy
My dress is white
Float on frost
Glitter at my feet
Stomach joins heart
Will I take off?
My head tilted to suckle sweet—
So far
My headband falls
I have vertigo
Like a baby staring at Mother
A smile
Skipping across silver grass
This could be my wedding night
Or a dream.
The house
Glowing like uranium glass
Neighbors must watch
My silly dance
And chuckle—sort of—
I bet you
Some of them want to join me
(They sip whiskey cream)
But are afraid to be thought of
As drunks
It seems.

Remember?

Everyone's gone to work
Hustling, rushed
Stab spoons of wheat
Into hungry mouths
Sugared words
Poured, sweet
But unthought
Out
Did you even taste July
In the raspberry you just swallowed?
And the kids off to school
(Temporary moment of sanity)
A breath
Think about that alpine meadow
You wanted to roam.
When did life get this busy?
When was the last time
You wrote a poem?

Swimming in a Glacial Lake, New Hampshire

From the viewing deck
we spotted a glacial lake
far-off and deep
clear and cold
a bright blue bowl—
it served the sky.
And I am not sure why
but we decided to walk there,
down deep descents with fatal vistas
thickest of woods:
spruce, moosewood maple, birch
—scent of balsam and then,
break of blue.
There it was,
sapphire hues—
holy as church.
We swam in the clear cold
lake water lapping
as far above a voice echoed from the viewers;
"Look, they're swimming....!"
We smiled and gave each other a nod,
then all went quiet
as we stroked out of sight
and did the metaphysical—
water blending with sky,
souls absorbed in God.

The Morning I Left for Your Wake

Ossipee's mountains were shrouded
with rain and low-gray clouds—
the lake's water black as coffee.
Here and there a ray of sunlight
lit the mountain pass in sea-glass green
(a bit of hope for me) —

Hobie Cats
jibbed
coral and yellow...
I prayed for you
remembering our last visit—
final hellos

and goodbyes.

Acknowledgements

"Once, I Sailed the Seas" and "What We Mistake for Monsters" appeared in *The Westchester Review*.

www.ingramcontent.com/pod-product-compliance
Lightning Source LLC
Chambersburg PA
CBHW081152090426
42736CB00017B/3289